TOOLS FOR CAREGIVERS

- **ATOS:** 0.6
- **GRL:** C
- **WORD COUNT:** 29

- **CURRICULUM CONNECTIONS:** animals, counting

Skills to Teach

- **HIGH-FREQUENCY WORDS:** has, let's, this
- **CONTENT WORDS:** animal, count, five, four, horns, many, one, three, two
- **PUNCTUATION:** exclamation points, periods
- **WORD STUDY:** long /e/, spelled ee (three); long /o/, spelled o (horns); long /o/, spelled ou (four); multisyllable word (animal); /ow/, spelled ou (count)
- **TEXT TYPE:** information report

Before Reading Activities

- Read the title and give a simple statement of the main idea.
- Have students "walk" though the book and talk about what they see in the pictures.
- Introduce new vocabulary by having students predict the first letter and locate the word in the text.
- Discuss any unfamiliar concepts that are in the text.

After Reading Activities

Ask the readers to look closely at each picture in the book. Why do they think these animals have horns? Explain that most animals have horns to help defend and protect themselves against predators. That's why many are pointy. What other features can they point out about the horns in this book? Which ones are long? Which ones are short? What color are they? Write their answers on the board.

Tadpole Books are published by Jump!, 5357 Penn Avenue South, Minneapolis, MN 55419, www.jumplibrary.com

Editor: Jenna Trnka   Designer: Molly Ballanger

Photo Credits: Gennady Grechishkin/Shutterstock, cover; anankkml/iStock, 1; Andrew M. Allport/Shutterstock, 3; Warmlight/iStock, 2mr, 4–5; phalder/iStock, 2br, 6–7; reptiles4all/Shutterstock, 2bl, 8–9; FLPA/Alamy, 2tr, 10–11; Chinnasorn Pangcharoen/iStock, 2tl, 12–13; Gordon & Cathy Illg/Age Fotostock, 2ml, 14–15; Iakov Filimonov/Shutterstock, 16.

Library of Congress Cataloging-in-Publication Data
Names: Gleisner, Jenna Lee, author.
Title: Horns / by Jenna Lee Gleisner.
Description: Tadpole edition. | Minneapolis, MN: Jump!, Inc., (2020) | Series: Animal part smarts | Audience: Age 3–6. | Includes index.
Identifiers: LCCN 2018042927 (print) | LCCN 2018043971 (ebook) | ISBN 9781641287012 (ebook) | ISBN 9781641286992 (hardcover : alk. paper) ISBN 9781641287005 (paperback)
Subjects: LCSH: Horns—Juvenile literature.
Classification: LCC QL942 (ebook) | LCC QL942 .G64 2020 (print) | DDC 591.47—dc23
LC record available at https://lccn.loc.gov/2018042927

ANIMAL PART SMARTS

HORNS

by Jenna Lee Gleisner

TABLE OF CONTENTS

tadpole
books

WORDS TO KNOW

five

four

many

one

three

two

HORNS

horns

Let's count animal horns!

horn

This animal has one.

horns

This animal has two.

8

This animal has three.

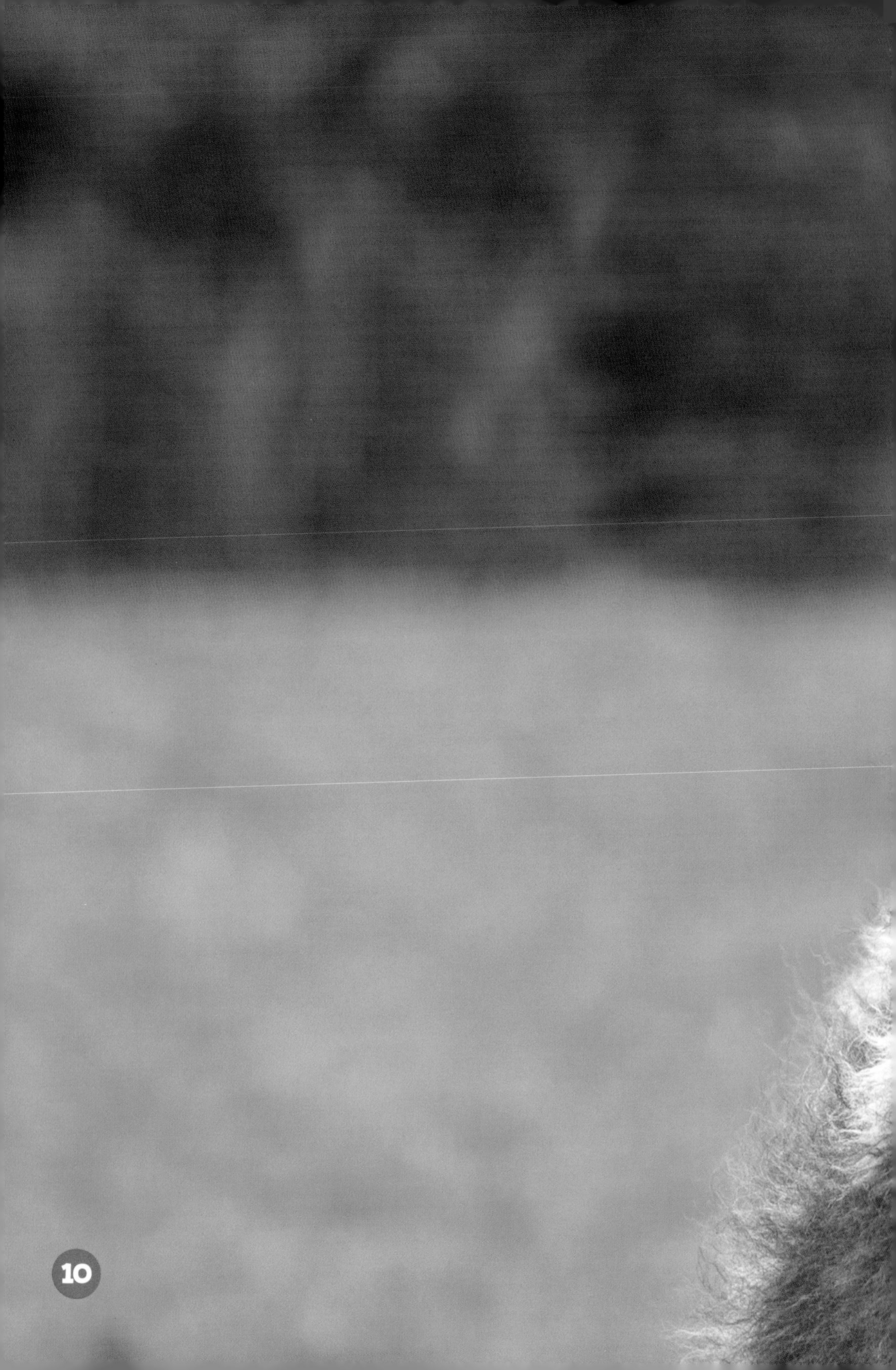

horns

This animal has four.

This animal has five.

This animal has many!

LET'S REVIEW!

How many horns does this animal have?

INDEX

16